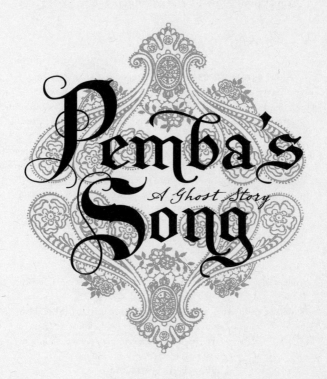

Pemba's Song
A Ghost Story

TONYA C. HEGAMIN & MARILYN NELSON

SCHOLASTIC PRESS/NEW YORK

To our dear friend Abraham, and to the
histories waiting to be uncovered. — MN

To our dear friend Abraham, for his courage
and commitment to reveal much Truth. — TH

Library of Congress Cataloging-in-Publication Data

Hegamin, Tonya.
Pemba's song : a ghost story / by Tonya Hegamin and Marilyn Nelson.
p.   cm.
Summary: As fifteen-year-old Pemba adjusts to leaving her Brooklyn,
New York, home for small-town Connecticut, a Black history researcher
helps her understand the paranormal experiences drawing her into the
life of a mulatto girl who was once a slave in her house.
ISBN-13: 978-0-545-02076-3
ISBN-10: 0-545-02076-X
[1. Parapsychology—Fiction. 2. African Americans—Fiction. 3. History—
Research—Fiction. 4. Moving, Household—Fiction. 5. Slavery—Fiction.
6. Connecticut—History—1775–1865—Fiction.] 1. Nelson, Marilyn.
II. Title.
PZ7.H35885Pem 2008
[Fic]—dc22
2007051044
Printed in the U.S.A.   23
First edition, September 2008

Book and cover design by Lillie Mear

Moving Day

Nothin' but trees. Miles of highway and nothin'
but trees. Mom's movin' me to Nowhere,
CT, when I used to live in the center of the universe:
Brooklyn, NY. This must be some kind of evil curse.
Who's gonna braid my hair?
I'm journalin' like my hand's on fire, earbuds blarin'.

My Urban Elf, Malik, hooked up
the bomb playlist for me. Yeah, I used to be a "we."
We met last year. Him always wearin' a crisp white hoodie
two times too big, hood always propped up.
I asked: "You some kind of urban elf?"
Teasin' cause I knew he was kinda feelin' me,
but boys like him ain't no guarantee.
Now how am I gonna make it by myself?

We used to lie under the trees in Prospect
Park; listenin' to music, watchin' the stars, chillin'.

Urban Elf told me: "One little state of mind
can't keep us apart." Or was that just a line?
There's a lot of trees between here and Brooklyn. . . .
Are there even any black people in CT?

⟡

"Pemba, take those things out your ears and listen," Mom says. "And don't poke that lip out at me."

I sigh hard and loud, press PAUSE on my MP3, close
my journal. She grips the steering wheel twice before
she continues, her knuckles turn white. "Look, I
know you're mad at me about this move, but I'm going
to need you to act like a young adult instead of a
child."

I can feel Mom looking hard at me like I'm going
to magically turn from fourteen to twenty-one in an
instant. I keep my eyes on the blurring green of trees
whirring past the window of our old station wagon,
which is riding low with our stuff.

"I've got this good job teaching near Hartford

that's better than any position I could get in the city and it's important to me." She talks like she's trying to convince me. I know what's important to *her* — but what about what's important to *me*?

"With this amazing deal I got on this house in cute little Colchester, we'll have so much more now. And when school starts back up, you'll have so many new friends. You'll like it, you'll see."

How could she assume what I'll like? Feels like lately she doesn't know me at all.

"You see, Pemba, there's a whole world outside of Brooklyn. This is a chance for both of us to move past the pain of losing your father."

Huh. I can't believe she's pulling the Daddy card on me, trying to soften me up. But I'm still not talking to her. I wish I was back home. My homegirls are probably hanging on Fulton Street right about now, acting foolish, cutting up, singing, doing some steps, showing off. Or else sitting on my best friend Raysha's steps, braiding hair. Or maybe going to the movies — my favorite thing to do in the summer. I like scary movies, mostly, especially when Malik and his boys would come, too. I liked to pretend I was scared so I can hug up on him.

Urban Elf would always say, "You can't be scared of some little ghosties! Not when you got me to protect you! 'Sides, ghosts never show up around black people — we don't take that kind of mess!"

"Girl, you hearing me?" Mom's getting mad now. I hiss back a yes so she'll simmer down. "I'm trying to do something better for us. You'll be in a great school, and I won't have to worry about you being in danger on the street."

Not that again! Just because some skank girls jumped me and Raysha for our gold chains doesn't mean we have to move all the way to the North Pole. Those girls were just some haters who couldn't afford their own bling. It's a shame how some people would do anything for money.

"Can I get your word that you'll try to be helpful and supportive?" Mom asks.

I mumble "whatever" and she cuts her eyes at me to say: *My patience is running thin.*

I push PLAY again — my music's all I have to keep me sane. I stuff the earbuds back in and go back to what will probably be my only other pastime from now on — tree staring. At least I can think about Malik, rapping chords and stealing kisses under each and every one of those trees.

For the rest of the long ride, Mom keeps looking at me, trying to get me to say something. I'm not talking till I'm good and ready. Or till she takes my MP3 away.

⚬

If you blinked, you'd almost miss all the cuteness of the quaint little town of Colchester, Connecticut. A tiny strip of stores, a supermarket, a rectangle of a park, a library, some old-looking buildings, and that's it. We get to the house and it looks a mess, like somebody forgot to remember it. It's old as hell. Not much more than a square with a pointed hat for a roof. Front and backyards need mowing (and I hope Mom doesn't think I'm the one to do it), a big, saggy front

5

porch with those old-time-y railings, peeling paint, and a huge tree out back that looks plain weary.

As Mom unlocks the door, I find a flyer on the porch: COME SUPPORT THE COLORED SCHOOL COMMITTEE. Colored school? Don't tell me they still have segregation up here! Like separate water fountains? I'm not having that!

I'm about to show the flyer to Mom as proof that we should turn around and go straight back to Brooklyn when an old man rides his bike past the house slowly, checking us out. He's neatly dressed in a short-sleeved, button-down white shirt and khaki pants. His dark, creased, round face looks serious. I wonder if he's like one of those Nation of Islam people. He cracks a grin when he sees me staring back. We're probably the only other black people he's seen in ages. *How country.*

He walks his bike up to the porch steps.

"Welcome, welcome," he says. "I must say, it warms my heart to see some fresh faces in our little town! My name is Abraham." He gives us a little bow.

Mom holds her hand out to shake his and introduces us in her bubbly "everything's wonderful!" voice. "We're looking forward to small-town living," she says, looking at me.

I suck my teeth.

"You all coming from the city? It'll be a big change, that's for sure," he laughs, like he knows something we don't. "But I'm sure you'll end up loving it here — most do."

I roll my eyes and don't stand around for the rest — let him and Mom talk about how great this nowhere place is.

I step inside and something about it — maybe it's the smell of the house — seems like it's been shut up a long, long time. And something about it feels heavy, too, like it's been holding its breath, waiting a long time to let it go. I move as quickly as I can, prying, cracking open windows and doors — the sound reminds me of when Raysha broke her arm in seventh-grade gym class.

The house is bare; there's layers of dust and a weird

goo on the kitchen wallpaper that's real thick. Before I can check out the upstairs, Mom comes in, looks around with her hands on her hips.

"Let's bring some life up in here!" she calls out while I roll my eyes. "I'll grab the mop; you get the sponge. Let's get to work!" She acts like she just found a genie lamp waiting to be rubbed.

We clean the house and move boxes in from the trailer attached to the wagon until late in the night. Our furniture won't come until tomorrow, so we have to sleep on air mattresses. Mom and I blow them up in silence. The *psh, psh, psh* sound of the pump makes me think of someone trying to keep a secret.

I almost ask Mom to stay with me — my room is kind of creepy with just one little lamp on the floor. There's shadows everywhere. I keep looking over my shoulder, feeling like there's someone there with me, watching. I'm not trying to punk out as easy as that! I'm from the city!

But tired as I am, I can't sleep, thinking about my Urban Elf and my friends, hating on Mom for bringing me to a place where my cell can't even pick up a freaking signal. It makes my stomach cramp. I try to console myself by thinking of all the messages I'll probably have on my voice mail in the morning. I'm so mad, my head throbs as the tears I've been fighting start soaking up the pillow. I haven't felt so lonely since Daddy . . .

I miss my life.

Attic Window
I was invisible when I slipped off upstairs
on the attic ladder. Nobody could find
me up there, where I used to seek you, Friend.
I'd steal a few minutes away from my chores,
and tiptoe back down when Miss Phebe called.
Dear Friend, you first came after my mami died
birthing my brother, the baby that died.
If it wasn't for old Master Hart, I would have been sold,
as not worth the bother.

Now Master Hart is gone.
I'm sitting on the splintery floor, hands in my lap,
asking you, Friend, to help me understand
how I live on, in the home of this wicked man,
knowing what I know. I don't really hope
for an answer. But it's good to be alone.

"Pem? Pemba!"

I hear Mom calling me through a fog of sleep, still feeling the weight of loneliness on my heart. I had such strange dreams. . . .

"Pemba!"

I don't even want to open my eyes; it's almost too much to bear, knowing I'll still be in some boring little town, missing everything I knew.

"Where are you?" Mom's yelling now but sounds like she's far away. I'm still not ready to open my eyes yet, but I realize I'm on the floor — the hard surface and close smell of musty wood tell me I must have rolled off the air mattress in the middle of the night. Hate these stupid things. I finally pry open my eyes, sitting up, but I end up banging my head on a low, slanted ceiling. How did I . . . ? Where . . . ?

"Mom?!" I call out. I feel so groggy, like I hadn't really slept. The whole room is covered in dust and cobwebs; a tiny oval window brings in a bit of hazy daylight.

"What are you doing up here in the attic?" I turn, and Mom is climbing a ladder behind me. The ladder I don't remember climbing to get here. Mom has to bend low to come in. I'm about to tell her I'm as surprised as she is when she claps her hands excitedly.

"Wow! Even more storage space! I'm so glad I kept your dad's old stuff! Now I have someplace to put it all — I forgot there was this much space. Good detective work, Pem!"

That's when I remember I'm not talking to her. I leave her up there with all her space and go down the ladder to my room, holding on to the rungs tight. I

11

hate ladders. I try to ignore my racing heart and shaking hands as I flop down on the air mattress, covering my head with the sheet. As soon as I shut my eyes again, I vaguely remember that dream . . . it was me, but not me . . . scared and lonely . . .

I throw off the covers, not wanting to think about it. I just want to talk to Malik. He'll make me feel better. Maybe I can convince him to come up here on the weekend instead of waiting until next month. I start scheming on how much I'd have to kiss up to Mom to get her to say yes.

I dress quickly. That dream I had sets my brain buzzing again. . . . I can't help but think she wanted something from me. . . . Hold up. *She who?* I tell myself to just shake it off; it's just this stupid place giving me nightmares. I probably was just looking for the bathroom, half asleep in the middle of the night . . . and somehow ended up in the attic? It didn't make sense, but nothing makes sense lately — except the sound of familiar voices. That's all I need.

I dress quickly, grab my bag with my journal, cell, and MP3 and run from the house yelling, "Be right back!" before Mom can rope me into some cleaning or unpacking. I find the library in town, next to the park. I can barely get a cell signal, even here. I go inside the library, looking for a pay phone when I notice that man, Abraham, sitting at a table, surrounded by books. He looks up and nods at me, and I nod back as I see the phone near the rear exit. I dial my voice mail quickly, practicing some of the new dance steps Raysha and I learned before I left.

The computerized voice stops me cold: *No new messages.* The old guy Abraham looks back at me just as I almost drop the phone. I turn away quickly and shove some more coins into the slot. I decide to call Raysha first. She and I have been tight since third grade and, as Mom says, we've been yapping at each other every day since.

"Why didn't you call me?" I demand as soon as she picks up.

"Pemba!" At least she sounds excited it's me. "Girl, I figured you'd be up to your neck in boxes by now."

13

She pauses. I can hear other voices in the background, the rush of traffic. She must be sitting on her front stoop.

"So what's it like there?" Raysha asks. "How's the house?"

"Ray, this whole place is whack — I miss Brooklyn so much! You couldn't fit half our 'hood up in here . . . and the house is a creepy old mess." She doesn't say anything. "What's poppin' down there?"

"My cousin KiKi is home from college. You remember her? She's here now, showing me steps she learned up there from the Stomp Squad. You're missing all the new hotness!"

I sure was. I knew I wouldn't be able to hold her attention for long.

"Hey, have you seen Malik?" I ask.

"Uh, Malik? I haven't seen him in a minute, girl. But I'm about to go up to Fulton Street Mall with Tisha to check up on the new Pumas. Maybe I'll see him there."

Tisha? That girl's always trying to copy me! Now

she's hanging with my best friend? I guess Tisha picked up real quick where I left off.

"It's all good, Raysha." I lie but can't help myself from blurting out, "Since when you hang with Tisha?"

"Aww! Don't catch feelings like that, Pem!" Raysha says quickly. "I gotta hang with somebody! You're the one with the new life and all — you'll probably be hanging with all those rich Connecticut kids soon, going to golf parties and playing croquet at the country club or whatever it is they do."

"Never!" I almost shout. I'm about to tell her about the crazy dream I had when she cuts in.

"Tisha's here now, girl. Holla at me later!" She's gone before I can tell her my cell isn't working. I hang up and sigh.

I have to call his cell, his mom's house, his dad's house, and then his cell again before I reach Malik.

"Yo, Shortie!" he shouts.

My heart flutters a little. It's hard to speak, I'm so happy to hear his voice. Music blares in the background. I can't tell if he's outside or inside, but I'm just glad to hear his voice. I can't help thinking about the last time we were in the park, all the sweet things he whispered in my ear. . . .

"Oh, Malik," I say, trying to talk through the lump in my throat.

"I tried calling you last night, the connection was unavailable or something," he says. The music gets louder and the sounds of a crowd shouting and laughing.

"I can't get a signal out here," I tell him. At least he tried to call. "I miss you, Urban Elf."

"I miss you, too, Shortie." His voice sounds muffled like he's covering up his mouth with his hand.

"Where you at?" I ask, trying not to sound like it matters.

"Me and Tobias just got out the train at Union Square, figured we'd run around Manhattan today,

16

trying to see what's what. So did you move in and everything? What's the place like?"

I tell him what Mom told me — movers come today but no cable, no Internet, not even a landline until early next week.

"Damn! You're really up in Jabip, huh?" he teases. His voice is muffled again and I hear him saying something to Tobias. "You and your ma talking yet?"

"Not yet," I say. "If you saw this place, you'd be mad at her, too." It's nice to hear him laugh. I slowly tell him about my dream, how I woke up in the attic. I ask him what he thinks.

He laughs. "Hold up, baby; what'd you say? I was watching some dancers. . . . Lemme call you back. . . ."

Cell Phone Blues

A heart drops on the dance floor.
It's a whack beat nobody can groove to.
Even the smoothest DJ would scratch that.
There's no music in this small town; no one to sing
my name. My feet are heavy, trippin',
missin' their usual partners.

I plug my ears with some loud sounds,
hopin' it'll help. But it's the city symphony
I'm wishin' for, rockin' me like harmony.
Voices, trains, traffic keep tempo. Phat bass rhythms
pumpin' all through me like some crazy drug;
ain't easy to shake out my system. Here,
my journal catches my tears like ink.
Plink, plink.

I'm secretly wishin' my friends were still cryin',
lost without me, heads in their hands,

waitin' for my call. I know it ain't right,
but I'm livin' in a house that feels nothin' like home.
Feelin' like my old life just got erased.
Feelin' like my picnic just got tidal waved.

⚬❈❈⚬

I don't know how long I'm sitting there in that park across from the library, writing in my journal, listening to sad songs when this Abraham comes and sits next to me like he's been invited.

"Everything all right, Sister?" he asks. *Who's his sister?*

"I don't really want to talk about it," I say, standing up and starting back toward the house. He actually gets up and walks along with me! Some people just can't take a hint.

"Sister, I understand this must be difficult for you, moving from the big city and all," he says with a very serious face. "Especially now with the new moon in Sagittarius and all — it can make people a bit crazy."

19

What kind of mess is he going on about?

"Listen, mister," I begin, about ready to ask him in the most polite way possible to leave me alone or I would tell my mom he's stalking me. But he just keeps talking right over me.

"Sister, I know it's hard because it was the same for me when I first moved from Chicago, before you were even born. And it's still hard! But I'm here now to tell you that if you keep your eyes and ears open, this town might have a lot more to offer than you think. There's a rich history here, you might be surprised. Like this project I'm working on . . ."

He reaches into his bag and pulls out another one of those flyers about the colored school.

"Mr. Abraham, like I already said — I don't feel like talking. I have to go help my mom unpack. Bye." I start walking ahead of him. He doesn't miss a beat keeping up.

"I'm not going to make you talk, Sister. I'm not in the business of making people do anything they don't want to. I'm actually headed up to your house, too. Your mama asked me to do some odd jobs to help get you settled. I just wanted to give you this, in case you wanted something to think about besides your own sorrows."

He thrusts the flyer into my hand and then walks ahead of me up to the house where the movers have already started unloading. Mom is standing on the porch, supervising. I really don't want to go back in there. My head hurts, and my stomach's a little queasy.

Mom greets Abraham while I drag my feet the rest of the way up the steps. I try to slink past her, but she catches me by the arm with a firm grip.

"I know this is a small town, Pem," she says in a lowered voice that means I'm in trouble but she doesn't want to yell in front of people. "But when you don't tell me where you're going, I get worried. Now get into this house, and try to be useful."

I yank my arm away. Sometimes she really gets on my nerves.

Inside, goose pimples raise on my arms, it's so cold. It must be eighty degrees outside, but in here it feels like forty. I run up the stairs, but something stops me at Mom's room. I hadn't noticed before the mirror built into the wall — my reflection catches my eye.

The mirror looks like it must be as old as the house. It's scratched in some places like someone scrubbed it with steel wool. But it's still pretty, with little hearts and flowers etched into it. I wonder how many other faces have looked in this same mirror. I peer closer at my hazy reflection; my face looks different, somehow . . . maybe because I've never studied myself so hard in the mirror when I felt so sad. But the closer I look, the stranger I feel. My head starts throbbing again. It's not just that I look sad; I don't look like myself at all. I want to look away, but something pulls me in and I can't stop staring into those eyes that are even sadder than mine. . . .

Master Bedchamber

Old Mistress Hart and Miss Phebe cared for me when I was a young child, and Miss Phebe could smile.

But her engagements seemed destined to fail:
One fiancé married another girl; one went to sea.
Side by side in her chamber, Miss Phebe and I
wrote with our fingertips on the counterpane
and ran across the hall when Mistress cried out in pain
from the front bedchamber, where she was preparing to die.
Minutes ago, after crooning and cooling her brow,
when she'd sunk again into a fitful sleep,
I had risen to leave, when her mirror beckoned to me.
I gazed and gazed into that mystery.

Mistress Hart just gave out a sigh so deep,
I know. Dear Friend, what will become of me now?

⟡⟡⟡

"You all right, Sister?" Old Abraham is shaking my shoulder. My heart is thumping like the floor at a step show. "You're looking kind of funny. Should I go get your mother?"

"No!" I say, looking back into the mirror where my face appears. "I'm . . . I'm fine. I just had a headache."

"Well, you looked mighty fixed, like you'd fallen into a dream."

He searches my eyes, but I turn away quickly, trying to hide my confusion, my fear. How could I begin to explain what just happened? Not even as easily as I could explain what happened to me this morning in the attic. *Oh, yeah, mister, I'm just sleepwalking and seeing other people's faces in mirrors, ain't no biggie.* I realize it's a good thing Malik didn't hear me when I spilled my guts earlier this morning — he would have broken up with me for sure.

"I was just daydreaming," I tell him, finding an interesting spot on the ceiling to stare at.

"Your mother asked me to pull down this old mirror before they begin to move in her furniture." He covers the floor with plastic and puts on some safety goggles and thick gloves, raising a big crowbar to the mirror.

"Wait," I say. "Who used to live here? Do you know?"

Abraham looks at me like he's curious and surprised at the same time.

"You mean, who lived here last? Hmmm, let me see now." He lowers the crowbar and leans on it. "Nobody's lived here for a long time. The Murphys were here back in eighty-one, but they didn't stay more than a year. Before that, it was . . . uh . . . them Flannigans. They owned the place for a good little while. Why d'you ask?"

"Did any of them have a girl about my age?" I ask. "Were any of them African American?" He gave me that same look again like I was a puzzle just out of the box.

"No, Sister," he replies slowly. "As a matter of fact, you and your mother are probably the first African Americans to own this house. I know for sure that the house was originally built by a man named Hart, way back in the 1700s. You don't mean back then, do you?"

"I guess not," I say. There couldn't have been any black people up here back then. I guess I really was just daydreaming. The name Hart sounds familiar, though.

"There's records in town, if you wanted 'em,"

Abraham says, raising the crowbar to the mirror again. I don't stick around to watch the glass shatter.

I spend the rest of the afternoon helping Mom unpack. It actually feels good to keep busy. I keep repeating in my head: *It was just a daydream.*

After a while I start to feel much better — no headache, not so freaked out. As the sun begins creeping back down to the horizon, I find my way up to my room to unpack my own stuff.

I find the box with all my pictures — Urban Elf's smile beaming at me on the top of the rest. He's so cute! I kiss the picture and put it right on top of my dresser. There are also pictures of me and Raysha in the fifth grade, trying really hard to look cool. On the back of one, it says: "Best Friends Till the End!" in Raysha's handwriting. I put those pictures next to Malik's.

At the bottom of the box is the framed picture of my dad in his military dress uniform, just before he died in the Iraq War. I've always kept it by my bed. I don't remember too much about him. Mom always says we were just alike. My cheeks feel hot as I remember how foolish I was after he died; I had a tough time getting over it. Mom even sent me to a shrink! I'm embarrassed to think about it now.

"Pemba!" I hear Mom call from the bottom of the stairs, her voice breaks through the music in my ears, takes me away from my thoughts. "Can you come down here for a sec?"

I find her on the front porch, sitting on the steps. She pats the empty space next to her. I don't want her to think we're all buddy-buddy again, so I sit down but not too close. I've got my MP3 player still on, but I take out the left plug so Mom won't get mad that we're not "interacting." She's saying how nice it is to sit on the steps without a whole lot of noise, people, and smelly traffic. I keep my mouth shut and just watch everything get dark. I miss the people, noise, and the smells of Brooklyn.

"I have to be at my new job all week, Pemba," Mom says. "I need you to be here to wait for the cable and phone people and to unpack and clean the rest of the house, okay?"

Damn! Sometimes she treats me like I'm some kind of slave! I smash a mosquito on my leg in response.

"I asked you a question, Little Miss Thing." Mom's voice is tight again. "I thought you adjusted your attitude problem with all the work you did today. I'm glad your father isn't here to see you acting like this."

I wish he was here so maybe we wouldn't have moved, I think.

The air is hot, buggy, and uncomfortable but not as uncomfortable as the silence between us. Suddenly, Abraham appears from somewhere inside the house, whistling.

"I'm finished clearing out the rest of those empty boxes," he tells Mom.

"Thanks so much, Abraham," Mom says. They start talking about that dumb Colored School committee meeting that he's always going on about.

"I think it's wonderful that you're trying to get recognition for such an important landmark," Mom tells him, like she's so impressed. They keep going on about some history junk, so I put my earbud back in.

Mom nudges me. "Don't be rude, Pemba. Mr. Abraham was just sharing some interesting stories about his life — how he was a Black Panther in the sixties. Why don't you go around back and get him a chair, so he'll be more comfortable."

Me? Why do I have to go get a chair when I'm obviously not interested in his story? But I know if I don't, Mom will make it the number one reason why Malik and Raysha can't come visit, even though she promised me they could as soon as the house was set up.

I take my time getting to the backyard; the air is so thick with heat. I notice that the lawn has been neatly mowed, by Abraham, I suppose. It sure wasn't Mom. Our backyard in Brooklyn was concrete, just how she liked it. The grass smells fresh and kind of sweet, even though it crackles under my feet from being so dry. The movers had stacked all the outdoor furniture by the weary tree standing back there. The tree's huge and old, probably as old as the house, maybe even older. Poor tree, even its leaves look droopy in this sticky heat. As I'm standing there, my head starts to throb again and my nostrils fill with a terrible stink.

Backyard Maple

The Easter joy of Miss Phebe's wedding day
streamed through the house, from cellar floor to roof.
But we soon knew Master John was virtue-proof:
He wanted to be somebody, and she was the way.
They were husband and wife in the eyes of God and man,
and brown-eyed Jared was born on Christmas Eve,
more beautiful than I'd known a baby could be.
Now I'm happily Mother's Helper, Miss Phebe's Right Hand,
though washing diapers is not my favorite chore.
Even less, since blue-eyed Ezra came so soon,
doubling my daily load of stinking cloth.

If I knew one, I would certainly whisper an oath
— or many! — scrubbing this kettle of diapers clean.
Dear Friend, do you think I'm destined for something more?

It takes me a moment to remember myself; I struggle to get back to the front of the house. My head feels like it was just struck by a bolt of lightning. Another one of those daydreams. My legs feel like I'm wading through a stream of gray jelly. I have to take a few deep breaths because my nose is still burning from that smell; reminds me of the time I helped Raysha change her baby brother's diapers after he'd eaten a whole box of raisins. Maybe I should tell Mom something is wrong.

"Pemba! What took you so long? And you didn't even bring the chair!"

She's already on my case as I turn the corner from the side of the house. Her tone tells me to keep my mouth shut about what happened in the backyard. She'd just think I was trying to get out of doing work or something. I straighten my back and swallow the lump in my throat like it's thick medicine.

"No, it's quite all right," Abraham says quickly.

"Thank you for the invitation, but I really need to be on my way." He wipes his head with a handkerchief. "Whew! It's mighty hot! Feels like a good storm brewing soon, don't you think? You feel that electricity bouncing around in the air? Causes strange things to happen."

"Mom," I cut in. "I have a headache. I'm going to bed."

"Abraham was just asking me about your name, Pem. Why don't you tell him the story?" Mom asks like she didn't even hear me say I have a headache.

"Why can't *you* just tell it?" I know my voice is whiny, but I can't help it. I just want to lay my head on my pillow, listen to music, write in my journal, and forget everything else.

"You don't have to tell me the whole story. How about just the meaning?" Abraham suggests.

"Pemba means the force of present existence," I say through my teeth.

"Interesting." He nods with his chin in his hand. "It suits you. Is it African?"

"I guess," I mumble. "My dad named me." I hurry back into the house.

I can hear Mom tell him as I climb the stairs, my tears threatening to spill over: "I just don't know what's gotten into that girl. . . ."

What's in a Name?

Chaos used to be just a vocabulary word
but now it's how I'm livin', *a condition
of total disorder or confusion . . . a vast abyss.*
Now how do I get out?
Wishin' my daddy was here won't help.
Not even the name he gave me keeps me sane.

He wanted me to remember the task at hand,
be a soldier's daughter. But I'm caught up
in the net of missing him, a helpless little fish,
feelin' like I got no force, no power of my own.
My present existence is gettin' kind of scary —
climbin' outta confusion ain't easy.
I never knew an abyss this deep
since Daddy stopped visitin' me. . . .

Wasn't it in my sleep? Or were they "daydreams,"
too? I struggle to remember,

but it just makes things worse.

What was that song Daddy used to sing?

Somethin' 'bout

everything is everything . . .

Mom's standing in the doorway of my bedroom. I close my journal and take out my earbuds.

"Can I come in?" she asks. I shrug.

"Abraham told me I should take it easy on you." She sits on the bed. "He said that this is such a sensitive time for you in your development as a young adult, and I should try to remember that." The side of her mouth wiggles in a tiny smile. "He also said that since you're a Scorpio, you're going to be moody and a little secretive sometimes."

"He said all that?"

She looks at me and we both giggle. "He sure is an interesting gentleman!" Mom says.

"He sure is."

That was kind of nice of him, sticking up for me

like that. Especially after how salty I've been to him. Guess he isn't too bad after all.

Mom nods and smiles again apologetically; this time I even let her brush a stray eyelash from my cheek. "He and I also worked out a proposition for you."

I raise an eyebrow dramatically. "Like what?"

"Well," she begins slowly, "since you're having a hard time adjusting to the new house and I have to be away most of the week, maybe you'd like to help Abraham do some research in the library instead of hanging around the house alone. He thought it'd be a good way for you to get to know the black history of the town."

"*Black* history? You mean that Colored School stuff?" I wonder if I was wrong to think there weren't ever any black people living here. "I'll think about it."

"Good," Mom says. "If you decide to do it, please just promise me that you'll stay in the library and not go running off god-knows-where. I like Abraham and he seems harmless, but we don't know anything about anybody here."

"Mom, if I can handle myself in Brooklyn, I think I'll be okay in a town that only has four stoplights."

Mom notices Daddy's picture on my nightstand. The curtains flutter lightly, dancing with a warm breeze as she picks up the picture and cradles it.

"I miss your dad so much" — Mom lets out a big sigh — "sometimes I think the memories I have of him are just a beautiful story I made up."

I scoot over, so she can lie down next to me. She looks tired and sad.

"I miss him, too," I say. I forgot Mom would be missing him extra hard lately; she spent a good part of the afternoon in the attic putting away his things.

"I remember how he used to hold me a lot," I tell her. "I remember the day he left in that huge green army plane — and how he cried almost as much as I did. I remember what he smelled like," I say as we both stare at his picture. "But I think that's because you kept a bottle of his cologne in your medicine cabinet for a long time."

"I still have it," she reveals with a smile. "It's nice for me to hear you talk about him, Pem."

"I remember how he used to sing to me," I tell her. "But I don't remember the song."

"Oh! I think I know — that old Donny Hathaway song — 'Voices Inside.'" I'm so glad she knows it. "It was his favorite; I'll have to bring down his old tapes and CDs for you. Maybe you'll find some more music to put in your thingamajig. Your daddy loved music, too," she says, about to get up. "Sometimes I think the only thing you got from me was stubbornness."

I hold on to her for a moment, making her stay.

"Mom — why'd you send me to that psychiatrist?" I want to know.

"You still remember that?" she asks, impressed. "I just wanted to make sure you adjusted to what happened to your dad. You were only ten and you got so confused. For a long time, you talked as though he were right next to you."

⊷≈⊶

It's finally dark outside. I break down and ask Mom to sleep in the bed with me. At this point, I'm not taking any chances. After hours, though, I can't sleep and now I have to pee. The house is full of sounds; before she fell asleep, Mom told me all the creaking noises I hear are just the house "settling." You'd think that after almost two hundred years it'd be settled by now.

With all the noise, I'm having a hard time getting enough courage to get to the bathroom. I keep thinking over and over about what Mom said about that psychiatrist. She tried assuring me it was just because I was a kid; that the doctor helped me get through it. I wish I could believe her.

I can vaguely remember the shrink's office. I think it had beige walls and brown couches. Sometimes the doctor would bring out toys for me to play with. The doctor was a tall, redheaded man — I think he had a mustache. I don't remember being afraid of my dad's death *until* I went to the shrink. I didn't really miss Daddy so much until . . . until the doctor repeated over and over: *Your father is dead. He can never come back.*

The memory makes me shiver, and my body reminds me to never again drink water before bed.

"Mom?" I whisper loudly. I nudge her a bit, but she snores in response. I already know it's no use; she always sleeps like a log. I feel myself settling into sleep, light at first, then deeper, until dreams start to come at me.

The moon isn't quite full, but it pushes enough shadows out of the way for me to make a run for it. My feet hit the wood floor with a slap. Mom lets out a loud snort and rolls to her side.

I make it to the bathroom by running but avoid looking in the mirror above the sink while I'm washing my hands. I don't want to see any other face but my own in there. My heart is thumping hard and fast like a bird's. I want to keep the light on as I leave, but, of course, the stupid thing blows the bulb. Don't I wish I'd thought to bring a flashlight! I take a deep breath and begin to run back down the long hall.

With each step I try to ignore my pressing headache, but the pain of it pins me in place just as I get to the top of the stairs, only a few paces away from my bedroom door. I hold on to the railing tight and fight the dizzy feeling. I sink to my knees, about to cry out to Mom, but the sharp pins of pain begin to lessen, so I open my eyes slowly. When I do, I can see straight down into the room Mom calls the parlor — it shimmers with a weird silver light, like somebody's left on a TV on one of those old black-and-white movie stations. The rest of the house is dark and quiet.

Something catches my eye — is it my imagination? What was that I just saw? I strain to see down the stairs, but I can't see much. Just some shadows from the trees, right? Instead of pain, now I'm paralyzed with fear — my muscles clench to my bones. Now my head feels like it's a giant ticking clock. I want to call out to Mom, but my throat turns into cardboard.

Did something just move across the floor? Relax, it could just be a mouse. A really big mouse. I'd be happy to see a mouse right now. Or is it

HER? The one from my dream? Maybe I don't want to know. Maybe I should just jump back into bed and hold the covers over my head.

The force of present existence . . . I'm in the present — nothing from the past can hurt me, right? I'm no punk!

I take a deep breath, and something in me pulls me to answer my curiosity. The first step isn't so bad. It creaks under my weight, so I tiptoe down three more steps just so I can see for sure. Did the temperature just drop, or is that chill coming from inside me?

The room glows with moonlight, casting figures in a weird way. It's almost like watching a messed-up television, like when the screen is full of static but you can still see the outline of the people in the show. None of them seems to notice as I peek into the room.

I can only see one side of the room where a young, but sad-looking white woman sits on a fancy sofa, reading to two young boys. They're all dressed funny, like that old colonial style. There is an old man sitting close to the sofa; he has a beard and sits in a comfortable chair, also reading. Something about the room feels heavy and pressing, it was like they were all sitting on something uncomfortable. A tall clock clunks the quiet moments away.

I tiptoe down two more steps, willing myself to see more.

In the opposite corner is a man who is young and clean-shaven. He rocks back and forth on the back legs of his chair, so he's partly in and out of shadow, turned toward the fireplace with a pinched face, pulling on a pipe.

I lean forward, looking for the girl whose face I saw in the mirror. She's there, sitting on the other side of the fireplace, her only light. Her head is bowed as she sews tiny stitches. The younger man isn't looking into the fire; he's silently watching the brown girl.

He's staring at her, studying her. She fumbles at her sewing, maybe she can feel his eyes on her? Something's strange about that man — something

that frightens me more than the fact that I'm seeing things that aren't really real.

The girl moves toward me; I'm too stunned to
get out of her way in time. She moves directly
into my path, almost moves through me, like
she's trying to pull me, unwilling, into her
world. . . .

Parlor

I'm not allowed to sit on the settee,
but I am allowed to pull my ladder-back chair
from the kitchen corner to the parlor fire,
for freezing evenings with the family.
Sometimes I listen when Mistress reads to the boys
— I like the story of Moses and the Promised Land —
but mostly my hands work, while I seek you, Friend.
I'm brought back by a scuffle's sudden noise,
or by Jared and Ezra being trundled off to sleep,
or by quarreling voices, or Miss Phebe's sniveling tears.

Into the basket of stockings I still must darn
go my mending or knitting, my needles and thread or yarn,
and I curtsy, excuse myself, return my chair,
and climb upstairs.

                         But just now, I heard a slap.

Mom stops the car in front of the library. "I'm so glad you're doing this for Abraham, Pem."

I'm really doing this for me — after last night there was no way I was staying in that house all day by myself.

"Are you sure you're okay?" Mom asks for the hundredth time that morning. She's looking very pretty in a new white linen pantsuit, ready to impress her boss. "Do you still have a headache?"

"No, I'm fine," I tell her while playing with the door handle. "Good luck today."

I don't want to lie, but how can I say: *Guess what, Mom! I had a paranormal experience last night!* on her first day of work?

She drives off; I watch the car merge swiftly into what I guess is the morning rush in Colchester's one major traffic intersection. The weather is already muggy, and it's only twenty to nine. Since it's still early for the library to be open, I try to get a signal on my cell phone. It's roaming, but I don't care. I'm able to get my voice mail — two new messages from Malik, just saying he missed me! I get another message from Raysha, wanting to know my address so she can send me some DVDs. I'm feeling the love now!

Just as I'm about to get my dial on, Abraham comes out of the library, talking about, "Ah-ha! My new research volunteer! Welcome!"

He ushers me into the building before I can even say good morning. The air-conditioning makes it breath-snatching cool inside; the building smells like unturned pages. Abraham sits me at a table already piled with books. I forgot to turn my MP3 off, the music streaming out of the earbuds dangling around my neck.

"May I?" Abraham asks, gesturing to my ear-

46

buds. "I'd like to know what it is you kids are always plugged into."

Handing the music over, I wince; I realize I'd been playing some Dirty South rap.

Abraham raises his eyebrow, barely putting the earbuds in before handing them back to me.

"Quite . . . enlightening," he says with a dead straight face. "Let's move on. I'd like you to begin here." He put a yellow lined tablet and pen on the table. "I'll be over there," he says, waving his hand in a general direction and disappearing somewhere in the back.

The librarian is just turning on the computers. She smiles at me pleasantly and continues her morning tasks. I check my watch against the library clock — five to nine. Guess Brutha Abraham gets here before the librarians do! I can't believe he just snatched me off the phone like that! I'm the one doing *him* a favor! But thinking about the headaches I got back in the house, and especially after last night, I realize I really don't have a choice.

Ghosties

Never thought I was the crazy type.

Never thought I'd lose it in one night.

Never thought ghosts might be real.

Never thought about this whole "psychic" deal.

Never thought about slavery.

Never thought about wantin' to be free.

Where do I go from here?

There's no one who could believe

much of anything I have to say;

they'd just point, laugh, or put me away.

Or worse, they'd tell me, "Don't be so naive."

But how can I forget that girl so sad and caged?

I gotta keep myself disengaged —

spend my summer as a volunteer.

I can keep them locked up in my windpipe,

my secrets only witnessed by moonlight.

I'll just be livin' in the present,

with all the excuses I can invent

to keep me from believing her story might be true.

Yeah, it'll be easy to pretend like I never knew.

Since I'd rather be writing rhymes in my journal, it takes me a while to get into the reading Abraham laid out before me, but after a couple of hours I'm glued to my seat, shocked to realize that there weren't just a few black people in Connecticut in the 1700s, there were *thousands*. Most were slaves. Way back in 1657, there was a big revolt up in Hartford — less than an hour away from here! But the most interesting thing to me was what they called the Great Negro Plot of 1741. A bunch of slaves almost burned down lower Manhattan!

I go through pages and pages about Africans who were enslaved even here up north — beaten, degraded, but some were free. My skin crawls knowing there were slaves in the North. That isn't what makes me mad; it's the fact that we didn't learn any of this in Social Studies class! I mean, damn, they hardly mention Harriet Tubman and Frederick Douglass and the Underground Railroad. Don't get me wrong, Harriet Tubman is my homegirl, but it's so messed up that there were so many people who did amazing things just for freedom, and now they were buried under the pages of unopened books.

I always used to think slavery only existed in states like Mississippi and Alabama. I wasn't even close to being right. It turns my stomach to find there were plenty of people who wanted slavery to continue in the North, even after the Civil War. Malik is always talking about "injustice," but I bet he didn't know all this!

I'm so hyped thinking about everything I have to school Malik and Raysha on that I don't even notice when Abraham appears, carrying another stack of books and papers. He sets them down, picks up my notepad, and reads the notes I made. It was tough to know what to write because all of it seemed so important.

"Impressive, Pemba." He hands me two more books, picks up the rest. I'm actually interested to find out what else there is to know. "This, of course, is just your preliminary study. You've only skimmed the surface so far."

"It makes me proud to find out what people did to get their freedom," I tell Abraham, "but it's making me a little nauseous, finding out all of the bad stuff." I groan.

"I bet — I had a lot of mixed feelings when I started doing this research, too. I had a lot of hatred, but I realized that kind of hate didn't do much. I had to start fueling myself with pride. We owe the ancestors that. So many of the souls who died in bondage just want us to recognize their struggles.

"But that sick feeling you're having . . . why didn't you just take a lunch break?"

I look at my watch; it was already one thirty.

"Ooh! I forgot lunch!"

"*Forgot* to eat? Sister, I could hear your belly talking from the other side of the library!"

Abraham giggles at library volume and goes off

51

again toward the back of the library. I stand and stretch. This library is really nice — cozy chairs and lots of computers. I've always liked libraries, at least when I didn't have assignments to worry about.

I look at my cell phone — no signal. I go straight to the pay phone, leave messages for Malik and Raysha since neither of them pick up. But it's okay. I've got so much to write in my journal, and my stomach is hollering at me anyway.

Human Bling

Supermarket checkout, my face all up in a magazine
when it hits me. An article about some of my favorite
hip-hop artists, pictures of some party in Manhattan,
everybody blingin', everybody dancin',
everybody with a drink in hand.
Somebody shootin' . . . somebody shot.

After what I'd been readin', thinkin' 'bout all day . . .
slavery, black people in chains,
that girl in my dream, she must've been a slave.
I wonder if she wore chains. In the magazine,
the playas and ballers were flossin' gold, diamonds
yanked out of Africa. I love my music, but
why's it have to be like *this*? I know the answer:
money and power. Same thing slavery was about.

Africans lived and died in the worse ways
for the same stuff we kill each other over now.

Some people do anything for money:
they'd kill a dream or sell a soul.
Chuck that magazine.
It was *so* not Hip-Hop.

I spend the next few days in the library with
Abraham, learning about Connecticut's slave history.
A week ago, I would've never pictured myself enjoying
spending the end of my summer vacation with my face
all up in a history book. Mom drops me off before
work, then picks me up at the library when she fin-
ishes in the evening. I take a lot home to read at night;
not like I'm sleeping much anyway. I haven't had any
of those major headaches for a day or two, but I'm also
learning to like the taste of iced coffee to keep me
awake. I e-mail Raysha and Malik from the library
computer when I get the chance, but Malik's computer
is at his dad's and his dad always uses it for work.
Raysha doesn't have a computer at home, so she only

checks it once or twice a week. But it feels funny to tell them what I'm doing, what I'm thinking about.

Wazup, Raysha?! Today I'm reading about a big plantation that had more than sixty slaves in a town not far from where we live. Abraham (he's this old guy I hang out with now) told me there were African burial grounds out in those woods. He says he'll take me out there when the weather gets cooler. Now Abraham has me typing up some of his research notes about the Colored School.

P.S. I think there's a ghost in our house.

I'm not really sure she'd understand. I don't think I would if I was her, either. I delete the e-mail and go back to working on translating Abraham's notes. It's like translating a foreign language because his handwriting is so funky! But I've had to figure it out, so I don't have to keep asking him to read it all to me.

This morning at breakfast, I found myself telling Mom about what I've learned.

"The school was started in 1804, and the first teacher was a man named Prince Saunders; later he organized the school system in Haiti," I said as I reached for more orange juice. "The cool thing is that the school was really supported in Colchester. A lot of other towns up north didn't like blacks coming in, even just to learn."

"The amount of Abraham's research sounds amazing," Mom said. "I don't think he was traditionally educated, either."

"I don't think if I went to college for ten years I'd learn as much as he's taught me just from his notes." I made the mistake of thinking out loud.

"You two make a good team," Mom said with a smile. "I always told you learning was fun."

"I didn't say it was *fun*. Just interesting." I didn't want her to think I was going to turn into some super brainiac nerd.

But some days I do really like it when Abraham builds a fortress of papers around me. It makes me feel safe, in a way, like everything I learn protects me. But I don't tell Mom that.

Abraham's trying to get the town to put up a historic memorial museum for the school. This time around, though, the town isn't so excited about the

Colored School. Abraham is working hard to get enough money together to pay for the building costs. We're supposed to put up some signs today.

I look at my pathetic cell and see that it's nine thirty already and I still haven't seen Abraham. Usually by now he's tossing books in my direction and asking me to look up something or the other on the Internet. I go ask a librarian about him; she points me to a little room in the very back. Abraham's name is handwritten on a card. I knock twice, there's a scuffling sound, then he cracks open the door. He looks sleepy but doesn't let me see in.

"Oh, yes. Pemba, I'll be out in a moment." He shuts the door. I go back to where I usually read and type, wondering about Abraham. *What's he doing back in that coat closet?*

"I apologize for being late. Thank you again for volunteering." He thanks me every morning. I'm just happy to get out of that house — still no cable, no phone, but we do have ghosts.

"No, thank *you*, Abraham. You have no idea . . ." I catch myself before saying anything else, but I'm sure he could see my face fall a bit — the tiredness was starting to get to me.

"Pemba, you look as bleary-eyed as I do this morning," he says. "Sit here, I'll be right back."

He comes back with two paper cups of coffee from where the librarians take their breaks. It tastes bitter and a bit like ink. We walk to the town green and sit down in the shade. The heat of the coffee actually takes my mind off of the stifling weather.

"Here's to secrets," he says, raising his cup, tapping it against mine. "I'll share mine first — just a summary, of course. There are some things in everyone's life that are meant to be kept private."

He sits his cup down and stands his two pointer fingers in a pyramid, and begins pacing back and forth in front of the bench, like he's about to give a well-thought-out speech.

"I almost grew up very happy," he begins. "I was a kid who loved school, loved learning. I didn't grow up with much; my dear mother and father worked hard sharecropping, but like most people back then, they lost a lot of what they had to the rich man who owned the land. My father was a noble man, and he felt he was being wronged. Hoping to find answers, he went to a Socialist movement meeting that was being held in a nearby house."

Abraham pauses, noticing my confusion.

"At that time, my dear, the Socialists were trying to recruit, organize, and empower people to vote for sharing the land and profits rather than filling the pockets of a few people; you understand?" I nod, not 100 percent sure, but he continues.

"The man who owned the land my family farmed found out about the meeting and sent the sheriff to check it out."

Abraham pauses to wipe his face and lets out a long sigh.

"Well, it ended in shooting, and although my father didn't even own a gun, he was killed, just for wanting his equal rights."

I can't help but think of my daddy, how much Abraham must have missed his own father growing up.

"I had to leave school almost as soon as I started,"

Abraham's voice cuts into my own sorrow. "I had to help my mama make ends meet, but we barely did and eventually we got evicted. We moved to Chicago where I worked hard for many years in factories, fixing things, whatever to make money. Soon I got interested in political movements. I got involved with the civil rights movement and in time made my way to Connecticut from Chicago to help organize here, to educate people about their rights, and still I could barely read."

"But after a while," he says, "I fell on some even harder times — found myself with no work. That's when I started coming to the library; devoted myself to reading. I ended up learning a lot, especially about Colchester."

He points out some historic places, tells me about the people of color who'd laid the town's foundations, even made the bricks.

"There were plenty of important, thoughtful people who graduated from the Colored School, so why shouldn't it be a landmark, too?" Abraham asks out loud.

"But after not too long" — Abraham's face changes as he speaks, but I can't name the expression — "I found myself needing a place to sleep, too. The librarians let me keep my things and a cot in the old AV room back there, I call it my office, since I was already working at the library every day."

Abraham looks at me and pulls his face back into a smile.

"They still fine me for late returns!"

I'm surprised he can make jokes about it. "So you *live* in the library?" I ask, knowing it's rude, but can't help myself.

"It's where I do my best work, so I'm happy until I can get my own place." His smile makes me relax, and so I smile, too.

The church clock chimes eleven times. We begin to walk back toward the library under the canopy of trees in silence. I'm not sure what to say. How can my crazy problems compare to his?

"So, Pemba," — Abraham turns and looks me in the eye — "what secret are you keeping?"

I try to play it off. "What secret?" I ask, staring at

my shadow as we walk into the light of the green man-icured lawn.

Abraham stops; I continue to study our shadows, their edges wavy from the rising heat. His shadow scratches its head.

"Well, let me see," he says. "A teenage girl from New York City who comes to the library all day, every day, and looks like she spent all night awake? That's not a girl with secrets?"

"The books you gave me are interesting," I say, which is true. "And the library is cool. We don't have air-conditioning at the house yet."

I can feel Abraham's eyes on me, but I'm steady keeping my eyes low, looking only at our dark shad-ows against the light-colored concrete. His shadow touches the tips of its fingers together.

"With all I've seen and been through, I hope you know there's not much that surprises me anymore."

I don't know what brought me to the breaking point, but as I clench my jaw and lift my head to give him the same line I'd been feeding Mom. *I'm fine, it's nothing.* I can't help myself anymore. Something says: *Let go,* and everything just spills out.

I tell him about the morning I woke up in the attic, the girl with the sad eyes in the mirror, and the creepy figures in the moonlight. I tell him what my mom said about me talking to my dad after he died. The only part that feels strange is when I start crying-telling him how much I miss my friends.

Abraham listens patiently as I ramble on and even leads me to a bench under a tree to sit down. When I run out of things to say, the sun feels like a spotlight on me, Pemba, the crazy chick. It's pretty embarrassing to blubber like a baby to someone you hardly know. But I feel so much better, calmer, after getting it all out.

"Well," Abraham says as though I only told him that I'd stubbed my toe, "first things first. Let's go see if you see her again."

"No! We don't have to!" I scramble for a reason. "I mean, nothing's happened lately, so maybe I really was just seeing things."

I don't know if he hears me or not, he just keeps walking. All I can do is tag along behind.

"With all of the solar flares lately, I should have known that there was going to be a unique psychic occurrence soon. Plus Virgo is retrograde this week," he says, mostly to himself.

I have no idea what he means, but he seems to be sure of what he's talking about.

"In order for us to find out if you're really psychometric, we have to test it," Abraham says. He walks so fast I'm almost out of breath keeping up.

"What?" I ask.

"Someone who can sense things just by touching an object," he says, like he's just telling me the earth is round.

Climbing up the front porch steps, Abraham asks in a very serious tone, "Do you feel any psychic vibrations here?"

I laugh out loud. "Psychic vibrations? C'mon, Abraham," I say.

"Whatever you like to call it, Sister, but I'm just trying to take this seriously because you seem to need my help; why don't you try, too?" He doesn't look like he's playing around, so I stop laughing and show him where I'd felt the other "vibrations."

"You know, something about you made me think you might be in touch with the fourth dimension," he mentions casually as we go through the house.

"Are you 'in touch with the *fourth dimension*'?" I ask.

"Oh, no," he replies, sounding a little disappointed. "I've just read plenty about it."

It was a relief to have someone in the house with me, sharing my secret, but it was disappointing when nothing happened.

"Guess I'm not so in touch after all," I sigh as we climb down from the attic. "I wish we'd never moved here."

"But then we would never have met, Sister. I mean

it when I thank you every day. You've helped me a great deal with my project."

That almost makes me feel better.

"Didn't you say you sensed something outside?" he asks.

"Yeah, it was like a strong smell. It was pretty gross."

"And did you see anything?" he asks. I try to remember; I'd gotten out of there so fast. . . .

"She was out by that big tree, with her hands in a tub of water, scrubbing something. . . ."

Abraham walks downstairs and through the kitchen with me close behind. As he opens up the back door, I feel a rush of cold air, almost like the library's air-conditioning. My skin feels clammy, moist, and my head is suddenly pounding like I'm banging it on the door itself.

Abraham turns, stepping onto the back porch and saying something, but it sounds fuzzy, muffled. I reach for the door to steady myself, but it takes forever for my hand to get there.

As I sink to the floor, I can barely hear Abraham's voice: ". . . her name?"

He looks back at me, his face twists in alarm. As Abraham reaches out to grab my arm, my legs feel watery, like they're flowing out from under me and my arms are lead heavy. Abraham is moving in slow motion, it's too late anyway; the floor is rising up to meet me. Although the sky is clear blue, I hear a sudden clap of thunder, the dance of rain on wood. Two men shouting, their voices sounding familiar, but it's what they say that makes me shudder.

Kitchen Doorway

Master Hart and Master John were squabbling again,
like roosters skirmishing in the poultry yard,
when I rushed in from marketing. Their words
were hard to hear, over the blowing rain
and thunder clash, but I did hear my name.

I nudged the door behind me with my hip,
put down my basket, and shook out my wrap.
"Phyllys shames us!" I heard Master John exclaim.
I heard Master Hart snarl something about
"... YOUR debt ..."
I pulled the door open and stepped back into the storm,
quietly closing the door. Then, rattling the latch,
I banged in, and stomped my feet on the mat.

The house is silent now, and toasty warm.
Do I shiver from menace, or because I am soaking wet?

⋅⋙❦⋘⋅

"I know it!" I hear myself say. Opening my eyes, I see Abraham's face looking down at me with concern. Pain is mixing some crazy beats in my brain. I'm a little groggy, but I realize I just fell in the kitchen doorway.

"Are you okay?" he asks. "Should we call your mother?"

"No!" I say, not wanting to worry her. "I think it

was one of those vibrations." I tell him everything I remember — mostly just voices, the two men and the wet cold.

"Her name," I exclaim. I try sitting up but it's still painful, since I fell right on my hip. ". . . it's Phyllys!"

Abraham's eyes brighten. "Are you sure? What was the time period? Are you positive she was of African descent? Did she say what she wanted from you?" He questions me almost in one breath.

"Slow down! Give me a second!" I get up from the floor with Abraham's help, still a little woozy.

"One of them wants to get rid of her." I try hard to remember more. Abraham leads me to a chair and gets me a glass of water.

"I don't know what the year was," I tell him. "But she was dressed like it was a long time ago. Kind of Pilgrim-y. And her skin was brown, but not very dark — like you can tell she's got something else in her."

"Something else?"

"Yeah, her complexion's kind of like my friend Malik's. I remember thinking that when I saw her in the mirror. Malik's dad is African, from Kenya, and his mom's from England." Abraham begins to pace the floor.

"What was it like?" he finally asks, peering at me as if I'd just disappeared and reappeared wearing a chicken suit.

I think it over for a second. "I can't really explain. I was there, but I wasn't there, you know?"

His shoulders droop. "No, but I wish I did."

"What did I do? What did I look like?"

"You fell, passed out, but it was only for a few moments. And you shivered as though you were cold."

Just then Mom comes through the front door, finding us in the kitchen.

"What are you two doing here, Pemba?" she asks, really annoyed. "I went to the library, but the librarians said you two left hours ago. What's going on?"

"Please let me explain," Abraham coaxes. "I think Pemba has been overexerting herself on my account. I've given her too much reading to accomplish and I think her sleep is suffering from it."

Mom eyes me carefully. "I thought I saw your light on late the last few nights."

"I'm fine, Mom," I say, wishing I could kick Abraham. He gives me a tiny wink.

"Yes, the librarians don't like it when people fall asleep on their books."

"Pemba!" Mom hisses. "I thought you were helping Abraham, not embarrassing him!"

"Oh, no! She's been extremely helpful — she was just complaining of a headache, so I wanted to escort her home."

"Another headache?" Mom's all concerned now. I didn't want her to worry. "Did you take anything? Of course not, I'm sure. Let me go find you something." She goes upstairs.

"What are you doing?" I whisper through my teeth.

"I'm sorry I had to lie," Abraham whispers back. "But you do need some rest. You've been through so much. You have to trust . . ." Mom comes back with a bottle of aspirin and makes me take two.

"Well," she says, a little calmer, "I came home early because the cable company said they'd be here by three o'clock this afternoon, and it's almost two o'clock already. Abraham, would you like to stay with us for an early dinner?"

He shakes his head and does a little bow. "Thank you, but I have a prior engagement I must get to," he says. "Pemba, please get some sleep so we can continue with our work. I'll do some digging tomorrow in the town records in regards to . . . your subject . . . while you're resting at home, of course."

He tips a pretend hat at me and says his good-byes.

"So this turned out for the best." Mom pulls food from the fridge. "You'll be here for the cable tomorrow."

Keepin' It Real

A moment inside someone else's head,
a time trick. Here I thought I wasn't good
at anything. It's scary to think of it —
how many lifetimes did she have to wait
between hers and mine, just for me
to say her name, to know her pain.

Now there's only time to sit and wonder
what happened to this Phyllys so long ago —
was she put on the auction block?
But just because I'm black, do I have a responsibility?
It's not like I can erase her captivity.
Where she is, there's no more slavery, no ticking clocks,
what is it she wants me to know?
Why do I have to suffer?

What would it be like to wear chains made of lead?
And here's something I never understood:

How could someone like her submit
and curtsy to people she must secretly hate?
I would've just run away . . . or maybe it wasn't that easy.
One thing's for sure: I can't let her existence be in vain.

⟞⟊⟞

I wake up to loud banging — I almost don't want to open my eyes. I'm in Mom's bed, but she's long gone. I slept with her last night as an extra precaution; running into ghosts at night isn't my idea of fun. Not that I slept much with all of her snoring. Daylight peeks out from under the curtains; I hear the banging sound again. At least this time it wasn't in my head; it was coming from downstairs. Pulling up the shade, I can see the cable van in the driveway — finally, TV! I jump the last three stairs and throw open the door just as the technician is about to drive away. She reluctantly puts the van in PARK and comes inside.

I'm geeked to see some television and to finally hook up my computer! I cross my fingers that I'll be

74

IM-ing Raysha and my Urban Elf by tonight! I run up to my room, get dressed, and begin setting up my desktop. Just as I'm about to plug it in, there's a crash like half of the house just came down.

The cable lady calls out, "Uh, hon? We've gotta problem down here."

I run to where she is in the kitchen, standing next to what used to be the kitchen wall adjacent to the parlor.

"What the . . . ! My mom is NOT going to like this." There's dust everywhere, covering the floor Mom had just waxed.

"See, it's all rotted plaster. I drilled just a bit, and the whole thing just crumbled. But you got yourself a nice new hearth!" She chomps on her gum with a half grin.

"Looks like the old fireplace was open, you know, to heat both rooms. Somebody covered it up, though. The rest'll have to come down, too, but that's a carpenter's job. Tell your mom to call us back when it's done."

Now I know what people mean when they say

"flabbergasted." I step over the rubble to close the back door behind her, but I see Abraham riding around the house on his bike.

"I've got some news," he says, leaning his bike against the house.

"Yeah, but first you gotta see this!" I have an idea as I lead him to our new open fireplace.

Taking a deep breath, I cross my fingers and whisper the meaning of my name as I reach out to touch the mantel. It pricks me with heat as though there's a fire already in it.

Hearth

Master Hart drains his cider and bangs home the cork.
He crosses the kitchen to the cellar door
and opens it. All of a sudden, an uproar
ignites like a grease blaze: Master John's loud bark.
"You wretch!" he shouts. "I shall have that money now!"
"I say she will not be sold," returns Master Hart.

I can't quite see, from where I stand at the hearth:
Was Master Hart pushed? Or did he fall somehow?

I run down after Master John. He is fish-belly pale,
the same as Master Hart, but HE is dead.
Master John's winter blue eyes pinprick into mine.
"It was apoplexy: Do you understand?"
"Yes, sir," I mumble. Master Hart's dear head
lies haloed by blood and cider. Now my life will be hell.

⋅⊰❦⊱⋅

"He's dead! He's dead! Look at all the blood!" I'm screaming. Even when I open my eyes to a frantic Abraham and no blood anywhere in sight, I'm still full of horror.

I'm dripping sweat and tears. I wipe my hands on my jeans a few times before I realize they weren't really covered in blood.

"Master Hart's dead!" I couldn't stop myself from repeating. Abraham mops my forehead with a cool damp towel to calm me.

I wanted to touch the hearth mantel at first; I wanted to know what would happen. But once I was in, it wasn't the same as before. Phyllys was stronger somehow, I guess that's why I saw everything, felt everything like it was so real. It was like she'd glued me to her, forced me to experience it with her. I couldn't get out until she let me go.

I know she wanted to tell me that man, her "Master John," wasn't just scary, he was evil.

I try to explain what I'd just been through — the two men fighting about money again, about selling Phyllys. She was scared . . . and then . . . it was all so bloody and frightening.

"What's apoplexy?" I ask Abraham when I can finally breathe normally.

"Something like a fit or a seizure," he says. "Is that how Hart died?"

I think again about what I saw . . . the frightening hatred in the younger man's eyes.

"That's what John told Phyllys," I remember. "But I don't believe him. And neither does she."

Abraham looks serious. "Sister, there's something

I have to tell you about all this." He's picking his words carefully, like Mom picks melons.

"I went to the county records. I found out that Ezekiel Hart, the owner of this house, did own a slave. But her name wasn't Phyllys. The only bill of sale was for a woman named Abby, and she was in her twenties. Hart owned her before he bought this house, a few years before he married."

My heart sinks like a tennis ball in tar. I was sure my visions were real, that Phyllys was real — I felt it. I know what I saw.

"It just means I have to do some more research," Abraham assures me when he sees the look on my face. "Especially after what I saw you go through today. I don't think you would have made that up."

I'm so relieved he believes me. I don't know what I'd do without him.

And he's right. There's so much more to this story. I get up, dizzy but ready. "Where do you think you're going?" Abraham demands.

"You think I'm staying here? We've got some studying to do."

Abraham doesn't try to change my mind. We walk over to the courthouse, near the library. It's a small, quiet building with blue carpeting inside. We go down to the basement reading room to find a table. The staff seem to know Abraham; they smile and whisper quiet hellos.

"I hang out here, too," he whispers.

After a lot of digging through papers we find a copy of the 1795 death certificate for Mr. Ezekiel Silas Hart. It's hard to read, but the cause of death is clear: Apoplexy.

Daddy's Girl

If this is true, if I can see ghosts,
then what about my dad?
Can I see him again? Talk to him? I try
pulling him out of the air with all my might. . . .
Nothin'.
I shed bitter tears, wipe them away quick.

There's someone who needs my help right now;
but how do I call out a murderer
who's already been turned into worm
fertilizer? What kind of justice does this serve?
How does he get what he deserves?
. . . or maybe that's not the question anyhow.
What about poor Phyllys, what happened to her?
How could she have braved this kind of storm?

She must've reached deep down into her innermost
soul to find that strength. Makes me feel kind of bad

how I pouted and whined. Without a cell, I acted like I'd die.
Can't believe I worried about everybody bein' white.
Phyllys only wanted a friend to take away the sting
of loneliness. That "Master" John makes me sick.

⸎

"Look!" Abraham comes back into the room in a
hurry, waving papers at me.

In his darkly lined hands is a property listing from
1792: Hart owned a house, forty-seven acres, two
horses, a carriage, and one mulatto slave named
Phyllys, aged fifteen. She was valued at about two hundred and fifty dollars.

"But why can't we find a bill of sale or birth certificate for her?" I ask. My hands are shaking to be holding
something that documents her life.

"Often there weren't birth or death certificates for
slaves," Abraham says. "Back then, it was more important how much they were worth. Besides, there are so
many lost records."

"Wait . . . what if Phyllys was Abby's daughter?" I wonder out loud. As soon as I say it, it feels right and familiar.

"Could very well be true." Abraham nods. "What do you think she wants from you?"

"Well, at first I thought she came to me because I was the first black person her age who'd ever lived in that house; or that we were both lonely there. I thought maybe she just wanted me to know she'd been there, too. But now I think she wants me to know Hart's death was more than an accident."

"But how do we prove that?" Abraham asks.

We're both silent for a moment, thinking; then I realize the bigger question.

"Abraham — it's not just Hart's death. We have to find out what happened to her after Hart died."

We do some more digging through the rest of Hart's papers and find the bill of sale for the house (and everything else in it) by Hart's daughter, Phebe, but mostly by her husband, John Brixton. By the time the house was sold in 1798, he'd even pawned off the washtub. But there was nothing about Phyllys, almost like she disappeared.

Something told me we had to go back to the house. I remember Mom talking about a tiny storage space behind her closet that I hadn't "felt" yet. I didn't look forward to going up there again, to what we might find.

The house still looks a little scary on the outside. It doesn't help that Mom's standing on the porch, hands on her hips and a sour look on her face. I cringe a bit, realizing I'd forgotten to call her or leave a note.

"Pemba, what has gotten into you?" Her voice is tight, and a large vein has popped out on her forehead. I bow my head, not even wanting to climb the stairs to stand next to her on the porch.

"I don't have any way to contact you, so you know I'm going to worry when I don't hear from you, then I come home and find you gone yet again. Meanwhile, there's a note from the phone company saying no one was here when they came, *and* there's a giant hole in my kitchen wall!" Mom's voice cracks as she stops to take a breath.

I notice Abraham taking slow steps backward in an attempt at escape, but Mom calls him out, too.

"Oh, no, sir! Both of you get in this house right now! It's about time for a talk." We march into the kitchen and sit at the table.

"Now, I know there's something going on," Mom says slowly, taking deep breaths and trying to collect herself. Abraham is studying the table closely, folding and unfolding his hands. I'm trying to come up with some kind of excuse for all this craziness, but nothing comes.

"I'm not saying it's good or bad, but I know it's something. And I deserve an explanation."

Abraham opens his mouth, but I stop him.

"You're right, Mom. I do owe you an explanation. Abraham's been helping me." I know she's angry and hurt, so I take her hand to soften what I'm about to say.

"I know you might find this hard to believe, but when I was little, I really did talk to Daddy. I really saw him after he died."

Mom's eyes get big with tears. I know she's scared

of what I'm saying because she doesn't understand. "Mom, I've seen another ghost, too."

She yanks her hand away from me, and her chair scrapes the floor noisily as she gets up.

"So this is what Abraham's helping you with?" I didn't expect her to get so angry. "Filling your head with *ghosts*? Making you believe in things that aren't true?"

Abraham speaks up. "Please . . . I'm sorry we've kept this secret about your daughter's gift from you."

Mom raises an eyebrow when he says "gift."

"But if you don't believe her after she explains everything, then I promise that I'll never bother either of you again."

Mom sighs long and hard but finally sits again and stays quiet while I tell her about the first night in the attic all the way up to the cable lady, the murder, and how we found information about Hart's death and the papers with Phyllys's name and worth.

She still looks skeptical. "I know you want to believe in all of this, honey, but there's no real proof. This John Brixton might be innocent. Maybe it was an accident," Mom says when I'm finished. "I think you're just caught up in all of this *history* Abraham has been filling you with." She makes it sound like he's been secretly poisoning me with knowledge.

"Then why's she still hanging around here?" I ask.

Mom pulls her lips in tight, still not convinced.

"We still haven't gone up the back stairs yet, Mom; I think there's a lot more to this story. Please — just come with us and see. If nothing happens, if I don't see anything, then you can send me to as many psychologists as you want."

Finally, she agrees. Abraham goes up first with a flashlight; I'm in the middle, crossing my fingers that I'll have another vision. Mom's clutching the back of my shirt.

I'm actually glad to know she's behind me; I'm afraid we'll find out something I don't want to know.

The staircase is creepy, hot, and close; there are spiderwebs everywhere, and it seems to take a hundred years to climb. As we approach the door, the vibrations grow stronger with every step, the usual headache and lonely heartache. Standing aside for me to enter, Abraham opens the door and it creaks like a tree in the wind.

Just as I step inside, tunnel vision darkens my sight; I can only see a tiny circle of light in front of me. My legs feel wobbly; it's hard for me stay up on my own. I reach behind me to catch Mom's wrist, try to warn her that I might faint. My voice can't get it together, though; the humming of a simple machine floods my ears. . . . The hairs on the back of my neck stand on end. . . . He's there. . . . He's watching. . . .

Spinning Wheel

I sit in the storeroom's stillness at the spinning wheel,
pedaling steadily, twisting and feeding the strands
evenly, with the rhythm of foot and hands.
He can't sell me now; he's too afraid I'll tell.
I know too much. He watches, watches me.
I twist and pedal. The spinning wheel spins and spins.
Yarn grows on the turning spindle, inch by inch.

"You are future dust," the wheel sings eerily.
Am I his slave now, or his prisoner?
Is the slave's silence a truth, or is it a lie?
How long must I live on with the torment
of fear, in this secret imprisonment?
My silence is heavier than the sky.

Friend, I'm filling that dreadful silence with the spinning
*   wheel's whirr.*

Mom's the one freaking out this time. Abraham tells me later that as soon as she saw me sink to the floor, she panicked. Luckily, Abraham was there to assure her I was okay, that this is how it happened before. The visions don't last but about a minute or two, so she didn't have too long to worry.

Phyllys had pulled me and held me even tighter than last time. It was like being pressed flat as a flower in the pages of a book. It's taking some time to bloom back into myself again.

Mom and Abraham help me back down the stairs; I feel very weak, more than from any of the other visions. Mom makes me lie on the couch in the parlor before she lets me talk.

"She's so scared of him," I begin weakly. "Even more than before; it's almost like she wishes he would sell her . . . but he's just watching. I think he's been keeping her in the house, won't let her leave." Remembering her fear, I drop my head into my hands. I shiver even though the heat has Mom opening windows. I feel feverish, my head's still pounding. The sky is dark and gray; I see a flash of lightning split open the clouds.

"Pem, I think I should take you to the hospital," Mom says, looking slightly frantic. "I don't know what just happened and I really don't care at this point, but you look terrible. You're making yourself sick over this."

I protest as much as I can, but I barely feel up to it.

"I don't mean to second guess a mother's intuition," Abraham says quietly, his fingertips touching in a little pyramid. "But perhaps if we just let her lie here for an hour or so and let her regain her senses, she'll be better. If not, we can always go to the hospital."

Mom reluctantly agrees. They go into the kitchen to let me rest and to make me some cool mint tea.

It's surprising how sick I feel. I never felt this bad before. I shiver again, even though the air is soupy thick. Lightning explodes again, followed by booming thunder. From where I lie on the couch, I can see the trees whipping their leaves around in the sudden gusts of wind.

I can hear Mom in the kitchen telling Abraham that she's going to call a doctor for me, no matter what. As weary as I feel, I think maybe she's right.

A blast of air sweeps across the room. I see my bag on the floor over by the coat closet across the room. I want my journal, so I can write about all of this before I forget.

Gathering all my strength, I pull myself up off of the couch to get it. The room seems slanted and uphill, but it's just across the room; I can make it. When I finally get there, I'm sweating like I just ran a marathon. I hold on to the brass knob of the door to steady myself and reach down into my bag. The knob turns with the weight of my hand, and the door opens just a crack. Rain begins to pound like jungle beats on the roof. I feel the energy drain out of me like I'd just been unplugged.

I come to, dazed and wasted. I hear voices, raindrops. It takes a lot of strength for me to open my eyes.

As soon as I do, paramedics are in my face, taking my temperature, pressing on my wrists, my stomach; asking me all kinds of questions, like what was the last thing I'd eaten, how much water I'd had to drink.

I can't think of anything except . . . "No . . ."

They put one of those oxygen masks on me, and I pull it off. I have to help Phyllys. I still feel so sick; my throat is sore and bone dry. I see Abraham standing next to Mom. I reach out to him.

"No . . ." is all I can struggle to get out. "No . . ."

Abraham touches my forehead. "Don't try to talk now, Sister. You've got to conserve your energy. Everything will be fine," he says kindly. "You just rest and get better."

How can I make him understand? I have to help Phyllys! She needs me!

Abraham pats my hand as the paramedics lift me into the ambulance.

"No!" I try to yell. Not much came out. Even if he heard me, I don't think he understood. Mom climbs in, crying, telling me to calm down. I try to take off the mask again, but one of the EMTs gives me a shot of something in my arm. They shut the doors of the ambulance. The rain is drumming steadily as the sirens call out, just for me. Out of the window, I can see the house getting smaller as we move farther away. Sleep weighs on me like chains.

⋅❧⋅

I wake up in a hospital bed, feeling sleepy and hungry. Abraham and Mom are chatting. They both get

93

up and come to my bedside. I take Mom's hand but wince trying to squeeze it; I notice there's an IV in the crook of my arm.

"Ouch!" There's a funny taste in my mouth, too. "What happened?"

Mom strokes my arm gently. "You were extremely sleep deprived and dehydrated, honey. You've been asleep for almost two days now. Abraham says he thinks you were up all week?"

Abraham hands me a cup of water. I drink it down slowly. There's so much that's just a blank in my head.

"I don't really know, Mom. I just remember reading a lot."

They both laugh, but it's not funny to me. I feel like I've got on mismatched shoes or something. There was something important.

"Where's my Shortie at?" a familiar voice shouts down the hall. Raysha, Malik, and Raysha's mom burst into the room, carrying bright flowers and balloons.

There's a lot of squealing, hugging, smiling; we introduce Abraham to everyone.

"How'd you guys know I was here?" I ask. I feel almost perfectly content with all of them around me. Raysha's mom brought a ton of plantains, beans, and rice — my favorite dishes she makes. There's still something nagging at me, though.

"Your moms called us," Malik says before he pushes a forkful of food into my mouth. He insists that he should feed me since I'm sick. I love it, but I can tell Mom is doing her best not to say anything.

"Yo, you don't know how scared I was when I picked up and it was your moms instead of you! I'd been burning up your cell for a few days," Malik says, eating more food from my plate than he's giving me.

"Yeah, me, too," Raysha says. "Didn't you get our messages?"

I shake my head no; my mouth full of sweet plantains and spicy rice.

"You left your phone at the library," Abraham says from his chair. "You're lucky I brought it — the thing kept ringing and ringing! I almost threw it across the room when I couldn't figure out how to make it stop!"

I had to laugh at the thought of Abraham wrestling with my cell, trying to choke it to death.

"I hope you don't mind, but I listened to all the sweet messages from your friends." Mom's eyes are bright with tears. "It finally dawned on me how much you all were missing one another, so I asked Raysha's mom to bring them. I hoped it would make you feel better."

"Thanks, Mom." I want to tell her I love her, too, but it's embarrassing with everyone around.

"We want to know what happened to *you*, girl!" Raysha's eyes squint with excitement.

I gulp down the last bit of my food. I rest my head on the pillow, trying to think. Everyone is quiet while I play with the little plastic name tag on my wrist. I feel like I'm disappointing them somehow.

"I can't explain it. . . ." I begin. "I remember working in the library with Abraham . . . I remember I had a lot of headaches lately. . . ." I look up at them all, hoping they can fill me in on everything I don't know. So much seems hazy and jumbled.

"Don't worry yourself about it now, Sister," Abraham says.

"You just need some more time to rest," Mom agrees.

But there is still something tugging at my brain. . . .

They release me from the hospital the next afternoon after poking and prodding me some more, saying I was extremely dehydrated and overly exhausted. At least I feel better.

When I first go into the house, everyone's watching me like I might spontaneously combust. I see my bag, still slumped in the corner by the closet. My journal is peeking out like it's been waiting patiently for me.

Mom stops me before I can go to get it. "You know, honey, if you don't feel safe or comfortable in this house, I will move us out right away. I don't care what it takes, we don't have to stay here with . . . well, with everything that's happened."

"Okay, Mom. Thanks," I say.

"Yeah — you just give the word, Shortie, and I'll be packing your boxes to move you back to Brooklyn!" Urban Elf wraps his long arm around me protectively and leads me to the couch.

"The problem is I still don't remember much," I sigh. My eyes wander back to my journal. "Maybe . . ."

Abraham follows my gaze. "That's just what I was thinking, Sister." He crosses the room and picks up my journal and holds it out with both hands, giving a little bow.

I open the book carefully, like it's worth its weight in gold. My whole body is tingling with anticipation. As I read the entries, the memories begin to slowly leak out of me. I remember how lonely and sad I felt, how confused I was. But most of all I remember Phyllys, my friend, the one who needed me the most.

Everyone kind of just stares at me while I retell what happened, my story and Phyllys's; some parts Abraham has to fill in for me. By the time I get to the part where I knew Phyllys wanted to be sold just to get away from John Brixton, everybody has tears in their eyes.

"Dag, girl!" Raysha finally breaks the silence. "You been through all that this week? I thought I had my hands full just having to hang out with that pain in the butt Tisha!"

"I told you that girl was whack!" I laugh, wiping my eyes.

"So what happened to Phyllys?" Malik wants to know. He kept his arms around me the whole time I told my story. By his voice, I can tell that he has no doubt in what I'd said.

"I still don't remember," I say quietly.

"You were over by the closet when we found you," Mom says. "Do you remember feeling the vibrations before you passed out?"

"I think so," I say. "I mostly remember feeling so sick, like I was about to . . ."

"Puke?" Malik offers.

"No! Like I was about to die."

"Okay, that's all I needed to hear," Mom says with

a frightened look on her face. "We're packing up and moving out. Everybody grab something. Let's go."

"Mom, wait a minute! I don't think *I* was about to die. I think . . . I think it was Phyllys." The thought dawns on me suddenly.

"Honey, I know you feel connected with this . . . ghost, and you want to know what happened to her, but I'm not risking your health any further. I can't bear it!"

"But I owe it to her to find out what happened!" I realize that I'm getting all worked up. But it's so important to me, bringing Phyllys's story into the light.

"I agree with your moms, Shortie," Malik chimes in. I look at him like he's crazy. "I know, but for real. Hear me out! You just got back from the hospital. Chill for a second before you go all ghost hunter on us, okay?"

Even Raysha and Abraham seem to agree. I guess I have to give in.

"Fine," I say with my hand on my belly. "Is there at least something to eat around here?" Everyone is anxious to feed me, to take care of me. I feel really loved. As we all start moving into the kitchen, I feel the weight of my journal in my hands.

"I'm just going to put my journal away," I mumble and scoot back into the parlor.

I can't help myself. I have to know. I reach for the closet door.

Corner Closet

I.

I feel as though I have faded from chestnut brown
to a sickly yellowish pallor, almost white,
all of a sudden, practically overnight.
Sometimes the room seems to go upside down;
sometimes I must sit for a moment to catch my breath;
sometimes I fairly weep with a headache.
Perhaps there's some medicine I could take,
but I think Master John hopes for my death:
No doctor has come.
                    This afternoon I fell
to my knees in here, with an armload of sheets.

As I revived, I heard a furtive sound
and saw Master John at the fireplace, looking around,
removing a brick, hiding a folded note,
replacing the brick, and tiptoeing into the hall.

II.
Replacing the brick and tiptoeing into the hall,
he quietly closed the door. I am alone.
What can I do? How can I make a plan,
a way to live on? I have grown so ill,
I feel the nearing of my journey's end.
Help me point out that murderer, Master John,
so when he dies, his infamy may live on:
That's all I ask of you and Life, Dear Friend.
Except for *THE HOLY BIBLE, JESUS, and LORD,*
I cannot read. Someone must find that note.
Yet, but for dark people I saw on market days,
illiterate as I, who would believe a slave?
Shall I die with huge truth throttled in my throat,
because I can only read five words?

III.

Because I can read only five paltry words,

I must take Master John's cruel secret to the grave with me.

Please, Friend: If there's time in eternity

for Justice, this house is a place to start.

For here was a great wrong done.

                    I opened the door;

my eyes met Master John's. Stifling a scream,

I curtsied, eyes lowered. "Phyllys! You seem

peaked, child. Later, I'll bring you some more

of that tonic." His mouth smiled; his eyes frowned.

"Yes, sir," I mumbled, and pulled myself upstairs

to my airless room. I fell on my narrow bed

and lay weeping. Oh, Friend, I shall soon be dead,

cursed with a life in which nobody cares

        if I live, or if I fade from chestnut brown!

May 22d 1795

I am writing in a dredful fear that someone may see this.

As soon as I have hidden this it maybe will pass.

This a turribel thing to feel and I hope no one may ever
*   feel it.*

As I turned around a little while ago I thought I saw
*   the old man staring at me out of the dark.*

It was turribel to hear the old man scream as I knocked
*   him down.*

It seam to me that I still hear him.

Will he always haunt me?

If anybody ever finds this, which I hope they never will,
*   they know how turribel I feel.*

John~~~~~

Friends of Gold

An old piece of parchment, folded so neatly,
but its edges crumble like so much shame.
My hands hold proof of the murder of Ezekiel Hart
signed in John Brixton's evil hand. Here's our truth.
What I can't get over, what just does not compute —
in his claim of forgiveness, didn't he think of Phyllys?

To him, she wasn't worth what he could sell her for;
with what she knew, no price was enough.
Her life for his sins, an easy exchange
with no one there to help her, no one to believe.
Amazing how our lives got so tightly interweaved;
I think back to her face in the mirror; now it doesn't feel
    strange,
we could've been sisters, I know she was tough.
From now on I'll think of her as my ancestor.

I know it's weird, but now I feel a kind of bliss

having this type of gift. And Abraham, that funny old coot,
is a blessing of a friend. He was there to soothe
my fears, coached me from whiny teen to lionheart,
so I could claim the real meaning of *my* name
and finally sweet Phyllys could call herself a *we*.

-⊶⊱⊰⊷-

Everybody was mad at me at first for totally going against their wishes by connecting with Phyllys again, but once I showed them the letter hidden behind a brick in the fireplace, they didn't seem to mind. Like me, they were all relieved that the mystery of Phyllys's and Hart's murders was finally solved.

A week later, the house feels completely different, like it's taken a sigh of relief. I touch all the old places that held memories, but there's no headaches, no sign of Phyllys. I feel like she got what she needed from me — a friend to know her pain. I almost miss her, but I'm happy to be able to breathe in my own house again.

Mom agreed to let Malik and Raysha stay for a few

days, as long as they also work to spruce up the house. It really helps having them around and it's fun, too. We're going to paint my room a warm sunny yellow with glow-in-the-dark stars on the ceiling. We'll take lots of breaks, so Raysha can teach me new steps while Urban Elf beat-boxes. Laughing and talking with them makes the house feel more like my home, too.

Of course, Urban Elf is still on alert.

"Shortie, you better let me go first, just in case," he says every time we go into a dark room. He makes me lie down on the couch when he sees me yawn or hold my head in my hands, covering me with a blanket even though it's ninety degrees. I can tell Mom thinks it's funny. Raysha just rolls her eyes. It might be getting on my nerves.

"Malik, I really appreciate your help," I tell him quietly, holding his hand when we have a minute alone to sit out back under the maple tree. "And I know you believe what happened to me was real, but you don't have to treat me like I'm a baby."

He straightens up, pulls his hood back. I can't help

but smile a little — I can see he didn't let anyone else do his hair while I was away. His cologne smells delicious; musky but sweet.

"Sorry, Shortie. I know you can take care of yourself. I just want you to know you can count on me."

I put my head on his shoulder and look up at him. The sunlight looks like a disco ball through the leaves above his head.

"I know." I touch his face. He leans down and our lips brush softly at first, but we press into each other for a moment before letting go.

"Listen to this," he says, putting headphones to my ears, still wearing a big grin.

The Force of Present Existence

Welcomed back by the Ancestors, you know
death is reunion, a circle made whole.
Yet when the living know you once were real,
when they revere your name, it is as though

the universe falls still for your solo,
and your voice soars, pure as lovelight.

                                  Thus heal

all of life's sufferings. Now an "angel"
(as the living call us), you can bestow
occasional miracles, that sort of thing.
But mostly we love, cross our fingers, and pray.

The Force of Present Existence, remembering me,
has been the Friend I was never able to see,
but whose love I felt until my dying day.
She speaks my name: I overflow with song.

photo by Carlo Halloway

This book came about from a chance meeting with a charismatic history buff named Abraham Hajj, who makes his intellectual home in the public library in Colchester, Connecticut. It was Abraham who brought authors Marilyn Nelson and Tonya C. Hegamin together in the creation of *Pemba's Song: A Ghost Story.*

Abraham himself appears in the book and is also key to bringing together the two girls in the story. What serendipitous intrigue! Much of this book is based on the history of Colchester, Connecticut. Here is the real Abraham, pictured in front of Colchester's School for Colored Children, also cited in the novel.